History Snapshots

The 1970s

Sarah Ridley

W

FRANKLIN WATTS
LONDON • SYDNEY

This edition 2011

Copyright © Franklin Watts 2007

First published in 2007
by Franklin Watts
338 Euston Road
London NW1 3BH

Franklin Watts Australia
Level 17/207 Kent Street
Sydney, NSW 2000

Series editor: Sarah Peutrill
Art director: Jonathan Hair
Design: Jane Hawkins

A CIP catalogue record for this book is available from the British Library.

Dewey number: 941.085'7

ISBN: 978 1 4451 0580 2

Printed in China

Picture credits:
The Advertising Archives: 11b, 15t. Bettmann/Corbis: 24t. Mary Evans Picture Library: 10t, 11t, 12, 13b. Bob Grant/Hulton Archive/Getty Images: 25t. Sally & Richard Greenhill: 9t, 13t. Aubrey Hart/Hulton Archive/Getty Images: 6. HIP/Topfoto: 15c. Hulton Archive/Getty images: 10b, 23t, 23b. Manchester Daily Express/Science & Society Picture Library: 26. PA/Topfoto: 21. Picturepoint/Topham: front cover, 19, 18t, 28. Popperfoto: 9b. Science Museum/Science & Society Picture Library: 17b. Science & Society Picture Library: 27. Selwyn Tait/Sygma/Corbis: 20. Time & Life Pictures/Getty Images: 14. Topfoto: 3, 22. Graham Turner/Hulton Archive/Getty Images: 17t. R. Viner/Hulton Archive/Getty Images: 16. Graham Wood/Hulton Archive/Getty Images: 24b.

Thanks to the following for kind permission to use their photographs in this publication: the Baker family 8; the Orbell family 8; the Ridley family endpapers, 8, 18; the Wigglesworth family 8.

Every attempt has been made to clear copyright. Should there be any inadvertent omission please apply to the publisher for rectification.

Franklin Watts is a division of Hachette Children's Books, an Hachette UK company.
www.hachette.co.uk

Wakefield Libraries
& Information Services

This book should be returned by the last date stamped above. You may renew the loan personally, by post or telephone for a further period if the book is not required by another reader.

Contents

A time of change

Your grandparents, and maybe your parents, will remember life in the 1970s. It was a time of change. There were strikes and power cuts, strange fashions and Queen Elizabeth's Silver Jubilee celebrations.

Date: 1971

Post piles up during a postal strike. There were thousands of strikes during the 1970s.

1970s timeline

1970 The *Apollo 13* space mission almost ends in disaster when there is an explosion on board.

1971 Decimal currency comes in.

1972 The miners go on strike for better pay. Many Asians flee Uganda to live in Britain.

1973 Oil producing countries raise the price of oil, causing economic trouble worldwide. This leads to power cuts and the three-day week.

1974 The first games console, made by Atari, is in the shops.

1975 Britain builds oil rigs to drill for oil in the North Sea.

1976 There is a drought (extremely hot and dry weather) in Britain over the summer. Punk rock music becomes popular.

1977 Queen Elizabeth II's Silver Jubilee. The first *Star Wars* film is released.

1978 The first video recorder goes on sale.

1979 One million people are unemployed. Mrs Thatcher becomes prime minister.

Family life

In the 1970s children often lived close to grandparents, aunts, uncles and cousins. At home, most families ate together around a dining table. Generally, families only owned one television so they watched it together.

Date: 1974

Families often met up for Sunday lunch, birthdays and other occasions.

Date: 1971

By the 1970s, most families had a television. Gradually people replaced black and white televisions with colour sets.

Date: 1972

Families had to use candles during the many power cuts of the 1970s. People planned ahead by eating early and boiling up hot water while the electricity was still on.

Be a history detective

- Ask your grandparents what was different about home life in the 1970s.
- Look at the clothes people are wearing. It is a good way of working out when a photograph was taken.

Homes

Many new homes were built during the 1970s, a lot of them on housing estates. By this time, over half of all homes had a washing machine and a telephone. Freezers were becoming popular too.

Sold – to the family in the photo. A lot of houses in the 1970s were built in this style.

Date: 1970s

Fitted kitchens became popular in the 1970s, often with patterned tiles.

Date: 1975

More women started to take on paid jobs in the 1970s. Many began to buy frozen foods, such as fishfingers, to save time.

Date: early 1970s

The bath, basin and toilet in this fashionable bathroom are all avocado (green). Other popular colours were coral pink and chocolate brown.

Date: 1970s

Be a history detective

- Ask your grandparents about their home in the 1970s. What has changed? What is the same?

- How is your kitchen similar and different to the 1970s one?

School

After primary school, children went on to comprehensive school, although there were still many grammar schools. You had to pass an exam called the 11+ to go there. Pupils often left school for good at the age of 16, to learn how to do a job.

Date: 1973

A teacher and pupil work together in front of a blackboard. The teacher wrote on the blackboard with chalk.

Children sit at desks. The lid of each desk lifted up so that the pupils could store their books.

Date: 1970s

This girl is ready for Brownies, a popular after-school activity. There was not as great a variety of clubs and classes to choose from as today.

Date: 1972

Be a history detective

- Compare the classroom photographs with classrooms today. What is different? What is the same?

- Do you go to Brownies? Has the uniform changed?

Toys and games

Children played outside more than they do today. At home, toys included Lego, Barbie and Sindy dolls, Action Man and board games. Some of the new toys were Space Hoppers, Star Wars toys, Top Trumps cards and the first games console, by Atari (see page 26).

When the *Star Wars* film came out in 1977, many toys based on the film followed.

Date: 1977

Children hoped to receive a birthday gift like this one – a Chopper bicycle. Choppers had a long seat and high handlebars.

Date: 1970s

The Space Hopper was a new toy in the 1970s. It was usually bright orange.

Be a history detective

- If your parents, aunts or uncles can remember the 1970s, ask them what their favourite toys were.

- Why do you think children played outside more in the 1970s?

15

At work

The 1970s was a time of trouble at work. Many workers went on strike – refusing to work – in 1972. Then in 1973, there was a huge increase in the price of oil, which put up prices. Factories closed down so some people lost their jobs.

Women and children support the miners' strike. The miners wanted better pay, as did many other groups of workers in the 1970s, including refuse collectors and postal workers.

Date: 1972

16

Rubbish piled up on the streets during the 'winter of discontent'. It was called the winter of discontent because many workers went on strike, including the refuse collectors.

Date: 1979

Date: 1975

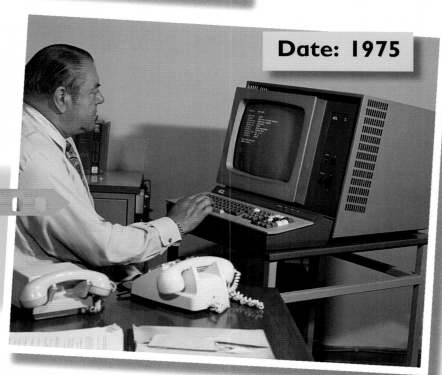

Computers gradually became much more important at work.

Be a history detective

- Ask your grandparents or parents what they remember about strikes in the 1970s. How did they manage?

- In what ways do computers and telephones differ from the ones in the 1970s?

Holidays

In the 1970s, cheap flights meant that more families could afford a holiday abroad. Then, on 7th June 1977, everyone received an extra day of holiday to celebrate Queen Elizabeth II's Silver Jubilee – 25 years as queen of Britain.

Date: 1970s

Package holidays, particularly to Spain and Greece, became popular.

Date: 1975

A family pose outside their caravan at a British seaside resort, which continued to be a popular choice for summer holidays.

Children wave Union Jacks during their street party to celebrate the Silver Jubilee. There were parties and fancy-dress parades all over the country.

Date: 1977

Be a history detective

- What food is on the table for the Silver Jubilee party?
- Where did your grandparents (and parents) go on holiday in the 1970s?

People on the move

In the 1970s, thousands of British people went to live in Australia, New Zealand or South Africa, searching for a better life. By contrast, 27,000 Asians came to live in Britain in 1972 to escape trouble in their home country, Uganda.

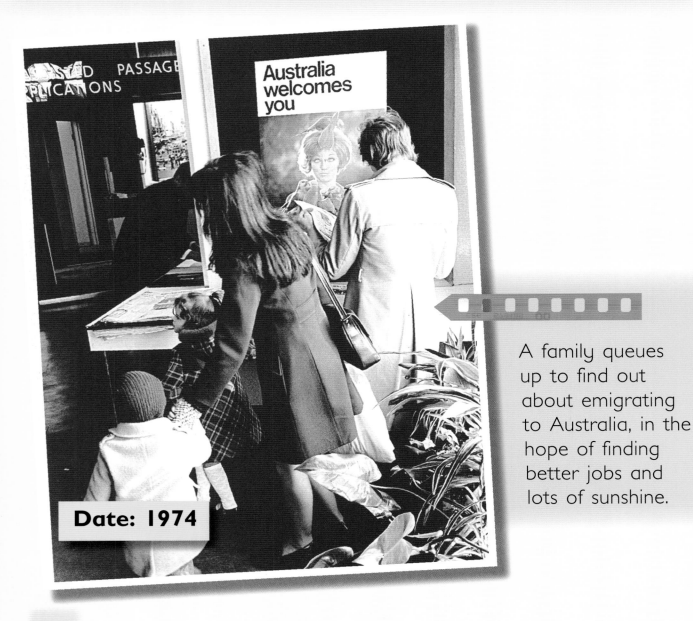

PASSAGE
APPLICATIONS

Australia welcomes you

Date: 1974

A family queues up to find out about emigrating to Australia, in the hope of finding better jobs and lots of sunshine.

Ugandan Asians arrive at a British airport. In 1972 the Ugandan president, Idi Amin, suddenly threw out thousands of Asians who held British passports.

Date: 1972

Be a history detective

- Do any of your family live in a different country? Find out why.
- For what reasons do people move to other countries today?

Fashion

It was fashionable to wear your hair long in the 1970s, whether you were a boy or a girl. Women wore short, hot pants one day, and long swirling skirts the next. Men and women wore flared trousers, called bell bottoms.

Extremely short shorts, called hot pants, were popular in the 1970s. Mothers dressed their children in brightly-coloured clothes, often with patterns or stripes on them.

Date: 1970s

The shoes this model is wearing are called platform shoes. Men and women wore platform shoes in the 1970s, although not usually as high as these.

One group of people, the punks, wanted people to notice that they were different. They cut up their clothes and added zips, belts and studs.

Date: 1979

Be a history detective

• What clothes do your grandparents remember wearing in the 1970s?

The seventies sound

Glam rock, disco and punk rock were all popular types of music in the 1970s.

Date: 1977

The film *Saturday Night Fever*, starring John Travolta (seen here), sparked off a big interest in disco dancing.

Bay City Roller fans wore tartan scarves in support of this Scottish pop band.

Date: 1975

Date: 1979

The Swedish band ABBA was extremely popular in the 1970s. People still listen to their music today.

Be a history detective

- Have you heard of the pop groups mentioned on this page?
- Ask your parents or grandparents to play you some 1970s pop music.
- Music was sold on records. Find out what these looked like.

Some 1970s inventions

Many machines that we take for granted were invented in the 1970s. The Walkman, the video recorder, the calculator, the digital watch and the games console all date from this time. Computers became much more powerful and smaller in size.

Date: 1977

Steve Heighway, a football star of the 1970s, plays Pong, using Atari, the first video games console for the home. Like modern games consoles, it plugged into the television.

Concorde, the supersonic airliner, soars into the sky. Concorde flew passengers between London and New York, USA, in just three hours.

Date: 1970s

Be a history detective

- Compare the Atari console with modern games consoles.
- Find out why Concorde no longer flies.

The change to decimal

In 1971, Britain changed over to decimal currency, the money we still use today. People learnt how to work out the value of the new coins in their head. See how fast you can work out the answers to questions A and B.

Old system:

12 old pennies = 1 shilling   20 shillings or 240 old pennies = £1

Decimal system:

10 new pence = 2 shillings   100 new pence = £1

A: How many shillings made 50 new pence?

B: How many shillings made 5 new pence?

Shoppers also used conversion charts, like the one this woman is holding, to work out the value of their shopping.

Date: 1971

Answers: A = 10 shillings   B = 1 shilling

Glossary

Comprehensive school A school for all or most of the children aged between 11 and 16 (or 18) in an area.

Decimal currency The money in use in the United Kingdom. The coins are counted up in decimals (tens and hundreds).

Emigrate To leave your own country and go to live in another country.

Fashion A style of clothes or other things that date from a particular period.

Fitted kitchen A kitchen where all the cupboards, shelves and surfaces are built to fit the space.

Grammar school A school for children aged between 11 and 18 that uses an exam to select its pupils.

Housing estate An area of housing and streets planned and built within a few years of each other.

Miner A person who works in a mine.

Package holiday A holiday abroad where the cost of the flight, accommodation and even some meals are included in one price.

Power cut When the electric power supply is stopped to a house or area. Many power cuts happened in the 1970s because the miners' strike caused a shortage of coal. Coal was burnt at power stations to make electricity.

Resort A seaside town or village popular for daytrips and holidays.

Silver Jubilee A celebration of the 25-year reign of a king or queen.

Strike A strike happens when workers refuse to work as a protest against pay or working conditions.

Unemployed Without a job.

Union Jack The flag of the United Kingdom.

Index

Further information

Books
When I Was Young: 1970s by Neil Thomson (Franklin Watts)
I Can Remember the 1970s by Sally Hewitt (Franklin Watts)

Websites
www.bbc.co.uk/cult/ilove/years/70sindex.shtml
Read about and see photos of the favourite toys, television programmes, music and films of the 1970s.

www.bbc.co.uk/cult/classic/bluepeter/lesleypetejohn/index.shtml
Information, photos and clips from Blue Peter in the 1970s.

http://news.bbc.co.uk/onthisday/hi/dates/stories/june/7/newsid_2562000/2562633.stm
Use this link to learn more about Queen Elizabeth II's Silver Jubilee celebrations in 1977.

Note to parents and teachers: Every effort has been made by the Publishers to ensure that these websites are suitable for children, that they are of the highest educational value, and that they contain no inappropriate or offensive material. However, because of the nature of the Internet, it is impossible to guarantee that the contents of these sites will not be altered. We strongly advise that Internet access is supervised by a responsible adult.